T0066981

Bioluminescent
Animals

THIS EDITION
Editorial Management by Oriel Square
Produced for DK by WonderLab Group LLC
Jennifer Emmett, Erica Green, Kate Hale, *Founders*

Editors Grace Hill Smith, Libby Romero, Michaela Weglinski;
Photography Editors Kelley Miller, Annette Kiesow, Nicole di Mella; **Managing Editor** Rachel Houghton;
Designers Project Design Company; **Researcher** Michelle Harris; **Copy Editor** Lori Merritt;
Indexer Connie Binder; **Proofreader** Larry Shea; **Reading Specialist** Dr. Jennifer Albro;
Curriculum Specialist Elaine Larson

Published in the United States by DK Publishing
1745 Broadway, 20th Floor, New York, NY 10019
Copyright © 2023 Dorling Kindersley Limited
DK, a Division of Penguin Random House LLC
22 23 24 25 26 10 9 8 7 6 5 4 3 2 1
001-334132-May/2023

All rights reserved.

Without limiting the rights under the copyright reserved above, no part of this publication may be reproduced, stored in or
introduced into a retrieval system, or transmitted, in any form, or by any means (electronic, mechanical, photocopying,
recording, or otherwise), without the prior written permission of the copyright owner.
Published in Great Britain by Dorling Kindersley Limited

A catalog record for this book
is available from the Library of Congress.
HC ISBN: 978-0-7440-7596-0
PB ISBN: 978-0-7440-7598-4

DK books are available at special discounts when purchased in bulk for sales promotions, premiums,
fundraising, or educational use. For details, contact: DK Publishing Special Markets,
1745 Broadway, 20th Floor, New York, NY 10019
SpecialSales@dk.com

Printed and bound in China

The publisher would like to thank the following for their kind permission to reproduce their images:
a=above; c=center; b=below; l=left; r=right; t=top; b/g=background

Alamy Stock Photo: Andrew Darrington 9tr, David Fleetham 17bc, PF-(usna1) 23b, Adisha Pramod 14br, Marko Steffensen 20,
VWPics / Kelvin Aitken 13br, Marli Wakeling 26cb, WILDLIFE GmbH 12-13t; **Alamy Stock Photo / Nature Picture Library:** 12br,
Kim Taylor 8tr, Martin Dohrn 15; **Ardea:** Paulo Di Oliviera 7tl, 23ca, 24cb, Dantâ"œÂ® Fenolio / Science Sour 9bl, 9br;
Dreamstime.com: Narint Asawaphisith 30-31, Dilyana Nikolova 6t, Seadam 16crb, Takuya Takenishi 7br;
Getty Images: Moment / Antonio Camacho 26br; **Getty Images / iStock:** E+ / tdub_video 4-5, Pinosub 15br;
naturepl.com: Jordi Chias 17bl, Doug Perrine 18br, Solvin Zankl 11cla; **Science Photo Library:** Dante Fenolio 1cb, 11bl, 21cb, 22cb,
27bl; **Shutterstock.com:** anko70 8b, Jukka Jantunen 25tr, Shaun Jeffers 28-29t, khlungcenter 8br, Photomann7 9cla, RobJ808 19bl

Cover images: *Front:* **Getty Images / iStock:** angkritth cra; **naturepl.com:** Magnus Lundgren; **Shutterstock.com:** Sorah Malka cla;
Back: **Dreamstime.com:** Fernando Gregory

All other images © Dorling Kindersley
For more information see: www.dkimages.com

For the curious
www.dk.com

Level 3

Bioluminescent Animals

Ruth A. Musgrave

Contents

ostracods, or sea fireflies

Cool Light

Flash. Flash, flash, flash.
Fireflies are having a conversation.

Fireflies glow. They are bioluminescent.
That means they make their own light.

Bioluminescent animals create light for
many reasons. They glow to communicate
with each other, find food and mates, hide
in the light, and warn off predators.

Bioluminescent light is cold light. Other
kinds of light, like from the Sun, a fire, or a
light bulb, all create heat. But the light of a
glowing animal is not hot.

Photophores
Organs on a bioluminescent animal's body create the light. The cells are called photophores.

Few animals living on land are bioluminescent. But more than 7 out of 10 deep-sea animals glow. That's because it's dark in the deep ocean. The animals use their glow to survive.

Let's shine some light on the animals that light up the dark.

Glowing Snails
Only one kind of land snail is bioluminescent. Its body has a soft glow. Scientists don't know why this snail shines.

Light the Night

Some kinds of insects glow.

More than 2,000 kinds of fireflies live throughout the world. Fireflies flash to find mates or to communicate with other fireflies. Their blinks might also warn predators that they taste bad or are poisonous. Different species of fireflies have different blinking patterns.

Click beetles may not look that flashy. But wait until dark. Then, this beetle's eyespots and abdomen glow. The glow of some click beetles can be seen from 100 feet (30 m) away.

click beetle

A Little Message
Firefly eggs and babies glow, too!
Like the adults, the little ones glow
to communicate a message
to predators. Their glow says,
"I taste bad."

egg

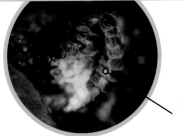

larva

Railroad worms are named for the lights
that run down both sides of their body.
The spots look like the lighted windows of
a train. Their glow helps these worms find
their way. Red eyespots adorn the railroad
worm's head, too. The red
lights frighten predators.

Hiding in the Light

Most bioluminescent animals live in the deep ocean. It is dark there all the time. Only a tiny bit of light travels down from the water's surface. Animals use this hint of light to hunt. They look up to search for silhouettes of animals swimming above them.

Prey need to hide their shadows to avoid being eaten by predators below them. They do this by making their own light. Bioluminescent light on the underside of an animal's body helps it blend into the light from above. Fish, squid, shrimp, sharks, krill, and other deep-sea animals use this kind of camouflage. It is called counter-illumination.

Many animals can even adjust the brightness of their glow. Then, they can move closer to or farther from the surface light and still be camouflaged. Some squid even change the color of their lights to match the subtle differences between sunlight or moonlight at the water's surface.

At 656 feet (200 m), little sunlight penetrates from the ocean's surface, and light completely disappears at 3,280 feet (1,000 m).

3,280 feet (1,000 m)

A firefly squid uses counter-illumination to hide (top). A firefly squid that is not emitting light (below)

13,123 feet (4,000 m)

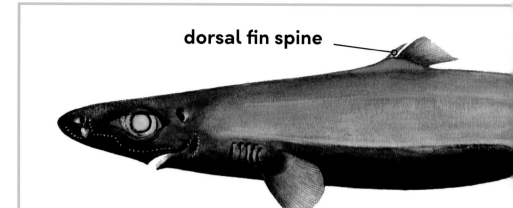

dorsal fin spine

Warning Lights

The velvet belly lanternshark has more than one way to survive in the deep sea.

   This shark's glowing underside helps it hide in the light from above. Animals swimming below it, including its prey, cannot see it. Part of its back glows, too. The light is so bright that the shark is visible from several feet (meters) away. A glaring glow like this is usually a lure to trick prey to come closer. But this shark's shine is a warning to stay away.

About 10 percent of shark species are bioluminescent. The pygmy shark is one of about 60 kinds of sharks that glow.

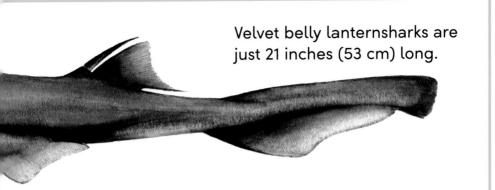

Velvet belly lanternsharks are just 21 inches (53 cm) long.

The spines on the shark's dorsal fins are transparent. That means the light shines through the spines. They look like lightsabers and warn predators to stay away.

Kitefin Shark
The world's largest bioluminescent animal with a backbone is the kitefin shark. It can be up to six feet (1.8 m) long.

Glowing Goo

Sometimes called sea fireflies, ostracods release a glowing goo to warn predators to stay away. If the predator ignores the warning and tries to eat the ostracod, it gets a mouthful of glowing slime. The gagging predator quickly spits out the little ostracod.

Male ostracods communicate with females by releasing bioluminescent, ball-like globs. They look like pretty glowing pearls. Each species releases the globs in a specific pattern and size. The globs are spaced a certain distance apart. This way, the right species of female is attracted to the display. The female follows the glowing row to find the male.

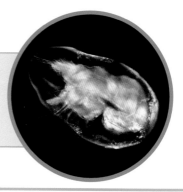

Ostracods
Ostracods are related to shrimp, crabs, and lobsters.

ostracod

glowing goo

Startling Shrimp

This deep-sea shrimp has a clever way to stop a predator in its tracks. It spits out a cloud of glowing goo. The light startles or blinds the predator. That gives the shrimp a chance to escape.

Shining in the Sea

Two types of jellyfish use their glow to warn away predators.

When a predator bothers the jellyfish, the atolla jellyfish puts on a spectacular light show. Lights circle its body and flash. Every animal nearby can see it. That is the goal. The jellyfish attracts attention so an even bigger predator, like a giant squid, will swoop in and eat the original predator. The atolla then makes its escape.

Jelly Bloom
Almost overnight, mauve stinger jellyfish populations increase by the thousands. These swarms are called a bloom.

The mauve stinger jellyfish has two ways to use light that might help it escape predators like sunfish and leatherback sea turtles. This jellyfish shines when startled. It also oozes bioluminescent slime.

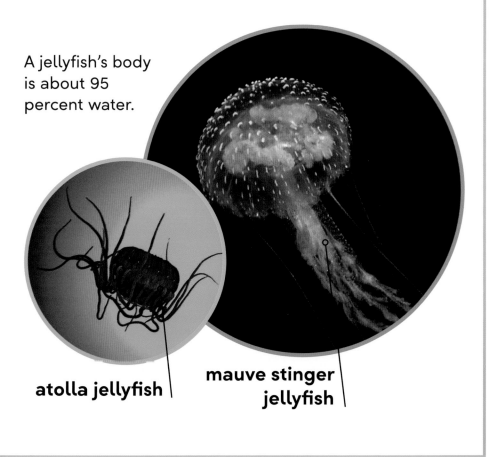

A jellyfish's body is about 95 percent water.

atolla jellyfish

mauve stinger jellyfish

Light Partners

Some animals don't glow it alone. They partner with bacteria. The animal provides a place for bacteria to live. Bacteria provide the glow.

Bacteria live everywhere on Earth. Most bacteria have important jobs. They help us digest food and help plants grow. Some glow in the dark.

The Hawaiian bobtail squid relies on one kind of bioluminescent bacteria. Glowing bacteria move into the squid right after it hatches.

Bobtail squid hunt shrimp at night. The bacteria provide the squid's glow on the underside of its body. The glow matches the moonlight at the water's surface, camouflaging the squid.

Some glowing bacteria want to be eaten. That's because they eat the digested food inside animals' stomachs. To get inside the animal, bacteria attach to ocean snow. That's tiny bits of floating dead animals, plants, and poop. It is a favorite food of many deep-sea animals. The glowing bacteria make the snow easier for animals to find.

Bobtail Squid
Bobtail squid are one of the few bioluminescent shallow-water animals. They hide in the sand during the day. The bobtail squid is about the size of a walnut.

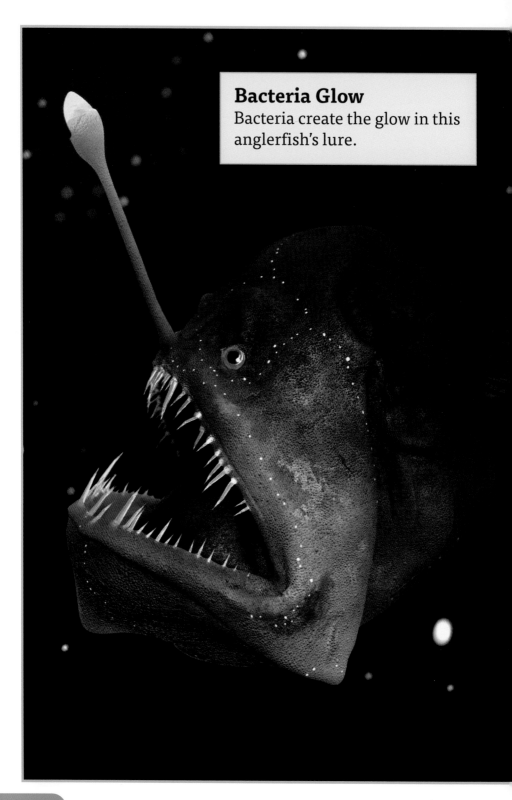

Bacteria Glow
Bacteria create the glow in this anglerfish's lure.

Trick of Light

Anglerfish use bioluminescence to trick their prey. The anglerfish wiggles what looks like a fishing pole in front of its mouth. The prey only sees the glowing lure at the tip. It looks like something yummy to eat. The hungry prey swims up for a nibble. In an instant, the anglerfish grabs and swallows its meal.

Baby anglerfish do not have a lure. As the fish grows, it moves slowly to deep water. Its body changes shape and the lure starts to grow.

Lights On, Lights Off

The dark ocean is the perfect place to shine. Thousands of flashlight fish swim together in schools. They glow to coordinate their movement. Flashlight fish also use their group glow to confuse predators, communicate with each other, and find food in coral reefs.

Flashlight fish are also called lanterneye fish. Here's why. A light organ under each eye is packed with bioluminescent bacteria. The fish rolls the organ out to flash the light. Then, it rolls the organ back in to hide the light.

Dragonfish
Most deep-sea animals cannot see red. Dragonfish have a red light that allows them to see in the dark water but keeps them hidden as they search for prey.

light organ

A flashlight fish can flash its lights 90 times in one minute!

A Dark Trick

The cookiecutter shark uses light to lure and trick prey, too.

Despite their small size, cookiecutter sharks can eat whales, dolphins, sea lions, and big fish. Well, not entirely. They just take a bite. But how do they get so close to such big animals? They trick them.

collar

Cookiecutter sharks feed on a dolphin.

bite mark

Cookiecutter Bite
This shark's name describes the hole that its bite leaves behind. It looks a bit like someone used a cookie cutter to remove the flesh.

Light cells cover the bottom of the shark from its chin to its tail. The only part that doesn't glow is the shark's dark collar. When a big animal looks up, it can't see the shark's body against the light coming down from the surface. But it can see the collar. That's the trick.

Scientists think that the dark collar looks like a small fish to bigger ocean animals. The prey swims up to try and eat it. The cookiecutter shark quickly latches onto the prey with its sharp teeth. Then, its whole body twists to cut out a plug of flesh, and it swims away with a mouthful of food.

Unusual Glowers

Meet the pyrosomes. These tube-shaped creatures glow. Pyrosomes range from the size of your thumbnail to some that are as long as four cars lined up end to end. Some pyrosomes are so big that a person could swim into the center of the tube!

A pyrosome is actually a colony of individual animals. The individual animals are called zooids. Hundreds to thousands of zooids live within the same jelly-like tube.

zooids

Pyrosome
A pyrosome might look like a kind of jelly, but it is more closely related to animals with backbones. Dolphins, whales, and some types of fish eat pyrosomes.

To move, eat, and breathe, the pyrosome takes in water from one side of its body. Each zooid helps move the water through the tube and out the other end. They filter microscopic food from the water.

Pyrosomes use light to communicate. Each zooid responds to light. That means if one lights up, the next one lights up, then the next. Nearby pyrosomes respond and light up, too. It is a mystery what information they are sharing.

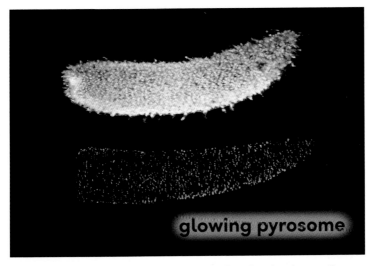

glowing pyrosome

Pyrosome means "fire body," which describes their bright glow.

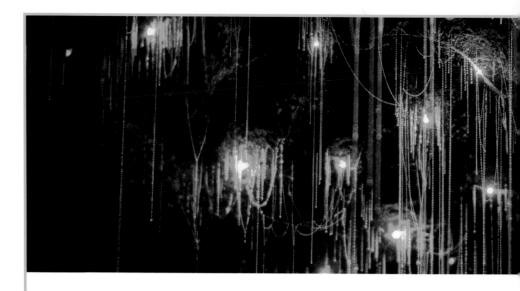

Light Show

The best light show on Earth might be in a dark cave! Thousands of glowworms glimmer inside caves in New Zealand, lighting the ceiling like a starry sky.

The glowworms are larval fungus gnats. The gnats live in damp areas near streams, in forests, and inside caves.

The glowworm builds a hammock-like nest. The nest hangs from the cave walls or tree branches. The larva makes and drops long threads called fishing lines. They have beads of glue-like droplets. The fishing lines

Glowworms
Glowworms eat moths, mayflies, midges, ants, millipedes, and even snails.

dangle below the nest, like a sticky curtain. The glowworm sits, waits, and glows to attract prey. Prey is caught in the sticky threads. The glowworm feels the prey trying to escape. It pulls up the fishing line with its mouth and eats its freshly caught meal.

From flashing fireflies to shining sharks, bioluminescent animals glow to communicate, to eat, and to survive. Scientists continue to discover more of these beautiful and fascinating animals. Which creature will be the next to show its glow?

Glossary

Bacteria
A single-celled microbe, or tiny living thing

Bioluminescent
(BI-oh-loo-mi-nehs-sent)
A living thing that can create light

Communicate
How animals share information

Counter-illumination
A type of camouflage in which the animal produces light to blend in with light coming from above

Gnat
A small, flying insect

Larva
Newly hatched or very young animals such as insects or fish

Microbes
Tiny living things that can only be seen with a microscope

Predator
An animal that hunts and eats other animals

Prey
An animal that is hunted and eaten by a predator

Silhouette
The dark shape of an animal that is created by light from the ocean's surface

Index

Quiz

Answer the questions to see what you have learned. Check your answers in the key below.

1. Which animal has lights that circle its body and flash?

2. Why do fireflies flash?

3. True or False: Bioluminescent light is hot.

4. What do bobtail squid hunt at night?

5. What lives in an anglerfish's lure?

6. Which animal hangs fishing lines to catch food?

7. What is another name for flashlight fish?

8. What animal only takes a bite from its prey?

1. Atolla jellyfish 2. To find mates, communicate with other fireflies, or warn predators 3. False 4. Shrimp 5. Bacteria 6. Glowworm
7. Lanterneye fish 8. Cookiecutter shark